# RUSSIAN REVOLUTION

*A History From Beginning to End*

BY

## HENRY FREEMAN

# Table of Contents

# Czarist Rule

*"Be Peter the Great, Ivan the Terrible, Emperor Paul.
Crush them all under you. Be the Master and all will bow
down to you."*

—Czarina Alexandra Feodorovna

By the turn of the 19th century, Russia had been ruled by powerful emperors for nearly four hundred years, with the Romanov family holding the throne with the ascension of Mikhail Feodorovich in 1613. The succession of Romanov family members to rule was convoluted and had often involved murder, conspiracy, and corruption, undermining the dynasty's legitimacy as hereditary rulers. International wars and internal revolts had plagued the country during these years, draining the economy, but also allowing Russian expansion in territory and power. Russia was in a continual state of financial disaster, exacerbated because of the lavish expenses of the Romanov court, which rivalled the courts of even the most prosperous European nations, England and France.

Russia had only recently emerged from four hundred years of feudalism, a system of government that required peasants, labelled as "serfs", to spend their lives working the land where they were born with little to no chance of ever improving their lot. Serfs were completely in the control of the landlord under laws that governed even the most personal parts of their lives. They were forbidden to leave the property of their landlord except under approved circumstances, could be told when and whom to marry, and could even be sold to another landlord. Czar Alexander II was facing growing disapproval from other European nations who had long dispensed with this framework of social organization and saw Russia as a backward nation both politically and economically. In response to this and increasing internal pressure the czar freed all Russian serfs by decree in 1861. He justified his reform to his critics by stating, "It is better to liberate the peasants from above" than wait until they win their freedom by uprisings "from below." Though the abolition of a system that had maintained a large percentage of the population as property was an improvement in the lives of the Russian peasants, the problem was more deeply rooted than a change from serf to peasant could rectify. The danger Czar Alexander II was attempting to prevent was more immediate than he realized.

Even after the abolition of feudalism in Russia, former serfs were required to continue working for their landlords as they always had for two more years. Then, the price of land available for peasants to purchase was artificially raised to preclude most peasants from ever owning their own land. Thus, most peasants stayed where they always had, doing the same work they had done as serfs. In spite of this, an influx of young Russian men and women took advantage of the new freedom of mobility to find jobs in urban factories. This migration to the cities brought about a phase of increased industrialization in

Russia, which brought improvement in the Russian economy in turn; unfortunately this also led to a new set of intolerable living conditions for mine and factory workers.

Czar Nicolas II, who was to become known as the last czar of Russia, ruled over a nation of growing discontent. In the twelfth year of the new 20th century, workers at a Russian mine in northeast Siberia took bold action that would initialize a wave of common feeling, changing their homeland forever.

Workers at Lena Goldfields mine along the Lena River were living in terrible conditions. They were forced to work fifteen hours a day or more in an environment that would be hazardous to even the most alert. Injuries were common with an estimated seven hundred accidents per thousand workers. Wages were low, and consisted partly of coupons that could only be redeemed at the company store. This only added to the profitability of the gold mine to its owners and investors, which included foreign nobility and the Russian royal family.

When the situation worsened to the extent that the workers were forced to use their hard-earned coupons to purchase rotten meat from the store, they decided to go on strike. Beyond the availability of edible meat, they pushed for fewer hours and other improvements to the working conditions. When the mine administration refused to consider their demands and arrested strike leaders, the workers marched with their complaint to the prosecutor's office.

They were met by the Russian army. Russian soldiers fired into the crowd of protestors, killing two hundred and seventy of the workers and injuring two hundred and fifty more. The divide between the common people and the Russian rulers was clear.

Worker's Rights, human equality, world war, murder, mysticism, blood and tyranny were to collide in the following decades to alter, irrevocably, the culture of this great nation.

# Karl Marx and Friedrich Engels

*"The history of all hitherto existing society is the history of class struggles."*

—Karl Marx

In 1848, German radical journalist Karl Marx had been expelled by the governments of Germany, France, and Belgium because of his radical writing. He collaborated with fellow German philosopher Friedrich Engels to publish a far-reaching political pamphlet, The Communist Manifesto.

The manifesto presents the argument that throughout history societies have been formed with the majority of the population living under the oppression of a powerful minority. The theory goes further to predict that these types of capitalist societies must, of necessity, eventually fall into class warfare and the bourgeoisie, or the upper-class minority, will be overthrown by the proletariat, or working class minority.

The short-term demands expressed by the manifesto include first, abolition of private property, free education, a progressive income tax, centralization of credit with a national bank, and nationalization of transportation, communication, and state-owned production. The end result of these demands was envisioned as a classless society where citizens would contribute based on their ability and receive based on their needs, with no need for the device of reward to compel the labor. The final paragraphs of the Communist Manifesto call for a united global action from the proletariat class to overthrow current governments. The text ends with the line, "Working Men of All Countries Unite!"

The Bolshevik leaders who rose to power during the Russian Revolution were all strongly influenced by Marx's work, including the Communist Manifesto. Vladimir Lenin, who would become the first chairman of the post-revolution government, based his political ideology and his contributions to the shape of the new government on his interpretation of Marx's writing. Lenin's own writing would spread and promulgate this view of social organization even further throughout his life. Because of the vast influence Marx's work has had on governments throughout the world, he is often referred to as "the father of Communism." Nowhere would Communist theory be as clearly expressed as in Russia in 1917.

# Nicholas Romanov

*"I am not prepared to be the Czar. I never wanted to become one. I know nothing of the business of ruling."*

—Nicholas II

Born in early 1868, Nicholas Romanov was the eldest of six children born to Emperor Alexander III and Empress Maria Feodorovna of Russia. The power of the Imperial government was already waning during his childhood, and the climate of revolution was heating up. When Nicholas was but thirteen years of age his grandfather, Czar Alexander II, was assassinated by an insurgent group intent on overthrowing the czarist rule of Russia.

On March 1, 1881, Czar Alexander II travelled to military roll call, as he did, predictably, every Sunday. Members of the terrorist group known as Narodnaya Volya, meaning "People's Freedom," were waiting for the czar's carriage at the point the route narrowed and crossed the Pevchesky Bridge. The first explosive that was thrown damaged the czar's carriage, killed one of his guards, and injured bystanders. It also had the effect of inducing the czar to leave the smoke-filled protection of the bullet-proof carriage. In the confusion of noise, debris, and panic, a second assassin threw another bomb, which exploded in the group of guards and police surrounding the czar. When the smoke cleared, Czar Alexander II lay in the street, hideously mutilated, covered in blood, with both legs torn away in the explosion. In this horrific condition, he was taken speedily by sled to the Winter Palace, where Nicholas arrived with the rest of the family. The czar died from his injuries soon after, with his son Alexander III and grandson Nicholas II at his bedside. The two future czars vowed to avoid his terrible fate. Nicholas's father Alexander III became czar after the assassination, and the young boy became Tsarevich, heir apparent to the Russian throne.

Ironically, the assassination of Czar Alexander II ended his plan to enact sweeping social reforms that might have satisfied the goals of groups agitating for the rights of the people. On the very day before he was killed, the czar had drafted a plan for creating an elected legislative body to represent the citizens of Russia. He had intended to release these plans the following day. His son, Alexander III, destroyed these plans when he became czar. The new ruler considered his father's murder justification for more brutal suppression of civil liberties instead of increased liberty. He is recorded as having vowed, "I shall never, under any circumstances, agree to a representative form of government because I consider it harmful to the people whom God has entrusted to my care."

The new administration was particularly hostile towards the Russian Jewish population. Czar Alexander III enacted a series of regulations called the May Laws, or temporary regulations regarding the Jews. Restrictions were placed on Jewish citizens preventing them from settling in certain locations, obtaining loans or mortgages, and transacting business on Sundays or Christian holy days. These "temporary measures" were to remain law for over thirty years. Beyond the punishing laws, violent riots aimed at Jews known as "pogroms" took place with the tacit approval of the czar. This culture of anti-Semitism would continue as an undercurrent in Russia, and would have tragic echoes throughout Europe in the first half of the century.

Despite his high station and the growing upheaval in his homeland, the future ruler of Russia spent his teenage years traveling the world. He visited family members in Europe, attending the royal wedding of his cousin the Duke of York in London, as well as touring Egypt, India, Singapore and Bangkok. An attempt was made to assassinate Nicholas while the group was travelling in Japan, causing the trip to be cut short. Nicholas's father, Czar Alexander III, refused to appoint Nicholas to a position in government, feeling his son was too young to take on the burden of such responsibility. Alexander being only in his forties, was a young ruler himself after the violent premature death of his father. Alexander assumed he would have years in which to prepare his son for the weight of the crown. Unfortunately, this assumption was proven false when Alexander's health began to decline. In 1894, the czar was diagnosed with terminal kidney disease. Though he received the best treatments available and spent time recuperating in the warmer clime of the summer palace in Livadia, nothing seemed to ease his condition. The czar was forty-nine years old when he passed away from his illness. Nicholas was just twenty-six, and he was the first to admit he was not prepared to take over as ruler of Russia.

Less than a week after the passing of Czar Alexander III and his ascension to the title of Czar Nicholas II, Nicholas was married. The bride was to his long-time love, Alexandra, a princess of Hesse and the Rhine, whom he had met at his cousin's wedding in London. Czar Alexander II had opposed the match prior to his illness, but relented when it was clear his health was failing. Alexandra herself had also had reservations about the marriage. She was reluctant to give up her Protestant faith in order to convert to Russian Orthodoxy, as would be required. After the encouragement of her parents, the princess marriage went ahead; the couple appeared to be devoted to each other.

The formal coronation ceremony for the new czar and czarina was held in 1896. The public celebration after the ceremony was held in Khodynka field outside of Moscow. It was a festival that promised feasting for all the citizens of Moscow. Unfortunately, a rumor was put out among the citizenry that there was not enough food and drink available for all of the celebrants. The crowd of approximately a hundred thousand people made a rush to get to the promised feast and trampled one another in the process. The end result of the panic was two thousand dead and injured at the celebration marking the beginning of Czar Nicholas II's rule. The czar's public image was damaged further when he was obliged to attend a state dinner hosted by French allies. His appearance at a dinner party only hours after the deaths was seen as callous and unfeeling. The tragedy was immediately interpreted as an ill omen for the new czar's reign, and only increased the distrust of the people.

Tragic events continued to haunt Nicholas's reign. In January of 1905, one hundred and twenty thousand workers went on strike in the capital city of Petrograd. The group hoped to present a list of their requests for reforms to Czar Nicholas II directly, so the workers marched toward the Winter Palace, singing the Russian Imperial anthem. The Winter Palace in Petrograd was a lavish Elizabethan-Baroque style building that had been the traditional home of Russian monarchs since 1732. Had Czar Nicholas II and the royal family not already moved to the Alexander palace at Tsarskoe Selo, or if he had given instruction to the minister in residence at the Winter Palace when he was notified of the planned march the night prior, it is possible the tragedy that followed might have been avoided. As it was, the peaceful demonstration was brought to an end on Sunday, January 22. The crowd of demonstrators in the square at the front of the Winter Palace was fired upon by the security police. It is estimated that a thousand men, women, and children were killed in the massacre. The disaster, which became known as Bloody Sunday, outraged the peasants and workers. In response, a wave of strikes and revolt swept the country. Worker's strikes took place in major cities, and peasant uprisings took place in the country. Even units of the Russian Army rioted along the course of the Trans-Siberian Railroad, threatening to disrupt primary transportation. The crew of the battleship Potemkin also joined the side of the revolt and mutinied.

In order to resolve the uprising, which became known as the Revolution of 1905, Czar Nicholas II was forced to institute extensive governmental reforms. The October Manifesto issued on October 30th was meant to appease the peasants and forestall further rebellion. The manifesto promised the establishment of a constitution and representation for the people in government by the formation of an elected legislative body called the Duma, meaning "deliberation." Many of the terms of the new legislation echoed the plan Czar Alexander II had been considering enacting twenty years earlier.

Neither the October Manifesto nor Nicholas' stated intentions met their promise. The first two sessions of the Duma were contentious and concentrated on gaining further governmental reform in favor of the workers. Instead of meeting this challenge diplomatically with the goal of coming to satisfactory settlement of grievances, Czar Nicholas II responded by dissolving the sessions without any agreements on reform being reached. The third session of the Duma, started in 1907, lasted the full five-year term prescribed in the October Manifesto by supporting government policy and only criticizing the worst cases of government abuses. Minimal progress in reform was made during this session. The fourth meeting of the Duma was also disbanded by Czar Nicholas in an act of desperation, but ended instead by accepting his resignation as ruler and establishing the first Provisional Government.

Czar Nicholas II ruled Russia much as his father Alexander II had. He strongly believed in the absolute autocracy of the crown. In hindsight, but also in reviewing governmental trends in Europe and the populist violence his own family had suffered, this adamant stance against popular representation in government seems hubris. This moment represents an opportunity when wiser leadership might have avoided much of the bloodshed soon to follow. Instead of considering the early proposal from a group of working class representatives pushing for a constitutional monarchy - a concession he would be forced to make anyway – Nicholas' firm rejection likely pushed the country one step further on the road to the revolution that would cost him everything.

# Rasputin

*"Our Friend's opinions of people are sometimes very strange, as you know yourself; therefore one must be careful."*

—Nicholas II

The Russian Royal family in the early 1900s included Czar Nicholas II, his wife the Empress Alexandra, his four daughters Grand Duchess Olga, Grand Duchess Tatiana, Grand Duchess Maria, and Grand Duchess Anastasia, as well as his only son and heir, Alexei. The young prince inherited a genetic disorder, presumably from his English mother, which was then known as "the royal disease," because of its prevalence in European royal families. Haemophilia B was untreatable at the time and usually lead to an early death for the afflicted.

When the finest doctors in Russia and Europe proved to be unable to help the young boy, Empress Alexandra turned in desperation to interviewing a long line of faith healers. It was at this time that Siberian holy man Gregori Rasputin became intimately involved with the royal family and thus the politics of Russia.

Gregori Yefimovich Rasputin is one of history's most enigmatic figures. Part sorcerer, part faith healer, part conspirator, the effect he had on the royal family and thus all of Russia is arguable and controversial. His motivations are suspect, but the truth of them is unknown. He is described as having a mesmerizing personality, and an entrancing stare. Many of his contemporary rivals ascribed his healing skills to the use of hypnotism on his patients. Many others believed he practiced dark sorcery.

After young prince Alexei was badly injured during a trip to the royal hunting retreat, he seemed to miraculously recover after Rasputin was consulted. The empress was so convinced by this chain of events that Rasputin became a welcome guest at court and a personal friend of the family. This favorable admission to the ruling family's inner circle was the beginning of Rasputin's reputation for mystic powers.

Modern doctors suspect that Rasputin's directive to limit treatment from the doctors at the time may have been the actual cause of Alexei's recovery. Aspirin had just come into wide use in medical treatment, and was seen as something of a miracle drug. Aspirin was likely a part of the prince's regular treatment from the royal physicians, but as the anti-coagulant property of aspirin was not yet known, the doctors would not have realized they were worsening their young patient's condition rather than easing it. Cessation of the administration of this drug may have been all that was needed for Alexei's condition to improve. The fortuitous happenstance of Rasputin's directives aligning with modern medical practice is a subject of debate among those who believe the legend of Rasputin's strange powers.

The Russian aristocracy had been involved in a fascination with all things occult for several years. The common people of Russia viewed this as highly suspect behavior, verging on blasphemy. Rasputin's close association with the Imperial family, along with his status as a holy man, brought public resentment against them.

When the czar took personal control of the war effort in 1914, Rasputin became even more influential with the empress. People feared that Czar Nicholas II would be killed in the war and they would be left to be ruled by Empress Alexandra as a puppet to Rasputin. Similar arrangements had previously occurred during Romanov rule, reinforcing the fear of this possibility.

Along with the undue influence he seemed to have with the empress and his reputed dark powers, Rasputin was also seen to behave outrageously when away from court. He was accused of drunken carousing, public indecency, visiting with women of ill repute, and even being a German spy. Rasputin soon became the most hated man in Russia, but Empress Alexandra remained his staunch supporter. Letters between Alexandra and Nicholas during this time refer to Rasputin as "our friend."

An assassination attempt was made against Rasputin in 1914. A woman wearing a black handkerchief to cover her face attacked him in the street and stabbed him in the stomach as he made his way home. He survived the attempt by running from her, covered in his own blood, with her chasing behind with her knife. He was eventually able to use a stick to beat the woman and defend himself. The woman, Khionia Guseva, was sentenced to a life of confinement in a madhouse, and Rasputin spent six weeks in the hospital in the care of the royal physicians. His recovery was seen as another example of his power.

In December of 1916, Rasputin sent a rather bizarre and ominous letter to Czar Nicholas II. In his letter he explained that he had a premonition of his own coming death. He declared that, if he was murdered by his brothers, the Russian peasants, that the czar and his children would reign in Russia for hundreds of years. However, if the czar's family was responsible for his death, they would themselves die within two years.

Fearing that Rasputin was exerting a demonic influence over the czar and his family and thus all of Russia, Nicholas's cousin, Grand Duke Dimitry Pavlovich, along with two other prominent men, planned to assassinate Rasputin. They invited him to the Yusupov Palace on December 30, 1916 whereupon they served him his preferred sweet wine and cakes all laced liberally with cyanide. When the poison did not immediately have the desired effect, Prince Felix Yusupov drew his pistol and shot Rasputin. With their target poisoned and shot, the men left Rasputin for dead and continued their evening. Amazingly, the injured man regained consciousness then fled the palace with Yusupov chasing him through the streets in order to shoot him a second time. Rasputin was still alive after the second bullet lodged in his back and the men threw his body into the freezing Neva River.

Several days after the assassination attempt, Rasputin's frozen corpse was found in the river. Prince Yusupov and the czar's own cousin, Grand Duke Pavlovich were exiled as punishment for the murder.

Whatever the truth of Rasputin's alleged dark powers, Romanov family members had taken part in his murder, and the first condition of his curse against the royal family was fulfilled.

# World War

*"All the horrors of all the ages were brought together; not only armies but whole populations were thrust into the midst of them..."*

—Winston Churchill

In June of 1914, Austrian archduke Franz Ferdinand was shot in the streets of Sarajevo, and the world went to war. Treaties and alliances between different nations meant that this act of terrorism from Serbia would by no means be an end to the violence. With seeming inevitability, nation after nation declared war. Austria-Hungary turned to its ally in Germany for support in punishing Serbia for the unforgivable crime. When Austria-Hungary delivered an ultimatum threatening military action, the Serbian government immediately requested assistance from its ally, Russia. Germany then declared war on Russia and started by attacking France, Russia's ally. With the violation of Belgian neutrality by the German army as their route to attacking France, Great Britain was obliged to enter the fray as well. Russia was drawn into the global conflict along with its European allies. By August, the growing anti-German fervor and battle-induced public patriotism were enough to overshadow the people's discontent with the ruling class and forestall worker strikes for a time.

Although it may have been impossible for any nation to be truly prepared for World War I, Russia certainly was not. A lack of necessary equipment and supplies plagued the army from the start. Along with thousands of men sent to the front without boots, ammunition or bedding, it is estimated that a third of the soldiers sent into battle were not issued a rifle. These unarmed soldiers were expected to obtain weapons as the opportunity arose and their comrades were killed during battle.

Foreseeably, the ill-prepared Russian army fared poorly in the Great War. Russia would lose more soldiers and civilians than any nation had in any previous war. Soldiers were conscripted to replace the thousands that had died or been taken prisoner, leading to labor shortages. The production and distribution of food and other necessities was negatively impacted across Russia. Worse yet, the war effort strained the nation's finances beyond breaking; inflation climbed to near four hundred percent. The continuous stream of defeats disheartened the country, and Czar Nicholas II, who had taken personal responsibility for the war effort, was held to blame. The people were poor and hungry, the war was humiliating and tragic, and the growing anger focused on Russian leaders, the czar and his family.

# 1917

*"From being a patriotic myth, the Russian people have become an awful reality."*

—Leon Trotsky

Against the backdrop of World War I and the terrible losses associated with it, the people of Russia were suffering. The food shortages brought on by so much of the nation's assets being dedicated to support the losing war meant people had no food. On March 8, 1917 demonstrators, primarily peasant women, took to the streets of the Russian capital of Petrograd demanding bread. They were joined by huge numbers of industrial workers already on strike. On March 11th, troops of the Petrograd army garrison were ordered to put down the uprising. Some of the soldiers opened fire on the crowd, killing protestors, but the people still refused to leave the streets. By March 12th, the soldiers of the garrison had defected to support the cause of the demonstrators, refusing to fire on the crowd when ordered to do so.

In the fallout that followed, the members of the Petrograd Soviet issued an order to take control of the Russian army. The Duma set up a provisional government led by Alexander Kerensky. On the day following the uprising, March 15th, Czar Nicholas II abdicated the throne for himself and Alexei in favor of his brother Michael. Michael in turn refused to take the crown. This led to the power in Russia being shared uneasily between the provisional government and the Bolshevik-controlled Petrograd Soviet.

The provisional government under Kerensky attempted to form the new Russian government as a republic, in accordance with the goals of the Socialist Revolutionary Party, but this move angered many who believed that the goal should be the gathering of a Constituent Assembly to determine the new course of government. The provisional government also determined to continue Russian involvement in World War I in spite of popular sentiment against the war. It was feared that withdrawal would negate alliances with European nations who were providing Russia with needed supplies. This decision was particularly unpopular among the military, who had assumed the new government would end their involvement in the losing war. Kerensky added to the feeling of disconnect in the army when he chose this moment to restructure the military chain of command and yet failed to address the abysmal deficit of supplies and morale.

Meanwhile, Bolshevik activists continued to agitate among the peasants, workers, and military. Bolshevik political meetings were held at factories to revolutionize workers. This group in particular had continuously been acting out in protest of the oppressive labor conditions, and were more than ready to embrace Bolshevik ideas.

In spite of the overthrow of the government and the abdication of the czar, the social and economic problems that led to the revolt in March did not improve. Soldiers left their posts and returned home in hoped of securing land for their families. Widespread raids on farms took place amid peasant food riots when the provisional government did not correct the food supply problems. The imperial government was replaced not by liberty, but by anarchy. This confusing and chaotic state of affairs would last for six months until an opportunistic new leader entered the picture in the form of Vladimir Lenin and the tempting Bolshevik party promise of "Peace, bread and land."

# Lenin

*"While the State exists there can be no freedom; when there is freedom there will be no State."*

—Vladimir Lenin

Vladimir Ilich Ulyanov was a young man headed to study law when his older brother Alexander was arrested on accusations of plotting the assassination of the Czar Alexander III as part of a radical group. His role in the plot had been to make the bomb that was to be used in the attempt. Alexander was later convicted and executed by hanging along with his co-conspirators. Influenced by Alexander's death, Vladimir began studying some of the radical ideas that had lead his brother to make his disastrous assassination attempt. When he arrived at Kazan University, he joined an agrarian socialist revolutionary group and became the elected representative of the illegal and secretive Samara and Simbirsk zemlyachestvo, a social club for men hailing from the same part of the country.

Because of his brother's conviction as a traitor and assassin, Vladimir was closely watched by officials around Kazan University. When he participated in a strike over a minor university student policy, he was arrested under suspicion of having been the leader of the protestors. As punishment, he was expelled from the university and forced to continue his studies as an external student. He now used his study time to read widely. He was particularly inspired by Nikolay Chernyshevsky's novel What is to be Done? and Karl Marx's book Capital. He was able to take his exams as an external student with the University of St. Petersburg and achieved a first-class degree with honors.

After graduating, Vladimir continued to participate in the Russian Socialist movement. He travelled around Europe to meet with other socialist groups, specifically the Emancipation of Labor group in Finland. A prolific writer, he created and distributed revolutionary pamphlets to factory workers. He collected illegal revolutionary publications from the European nations he visited and smuggled them back into Russia for distribution. For his work, he earned a high-ranking position in the Social Democrats group.

Vladimir was eventually arrested and charged with sedition for his involvement with a socialist propaganda piece, The Worker's Cause. After waiting a year in prison for his sentencing and cursory trial, he was finally exiled to Siberia. In exile, he continued writing political pamphlets anonymously and under many pseudonyms. Most notably, this is when he began using the name Lenin, under which he would achieve his greatest success. This was also the time when Lenin's beliefs on socialist philosophy diverted from the teachings of Karl Marx. While Marx had predicted a middle-class revolution as a necessary precursor to a socialist revolution of the working class proletariat, Lenin was convinced the workers of Russia could successfully throw off the

Imperial regime without rebellion in the middle-class. He was also convinced he could speed the process.

When The Great War broke out in 1914, Lenin was traveling in Galicia, in the Austro-Hungarian Empire. As a Russian citizen he was briefly imprisoned under suspicion of working for the Russian government, but was released when his anti-regime history was established. He was vehemently against Russia's involvement in the war. He viewed the situation as a petty and costly grasp for territory on the part of the nations involved; "a bourgeois lie."

After the people's uprising in 1917 that resulted in the abdication of the throne by Czar Nicholas II, Lenin returned to Petrograd to take part in the revolt. He was travelling with several members of the Bolshevik, which simply means "the majority" Party. As a revolutionary who would hopefully cause problems for one of their enemies, he was given a special pass by the German government that allowed Lenin and his fellow Bolsheviks passage through war-torn Germany and into Russia.

Immediately upon arriving in Petrograd, Lenin famously gave a speech at the Petrograd train station calling for a proletariat revolution to replace the provisional government. He became a well-known figure at radical meetings around Petrograd, belittling political rivals, the Mensheviks, as well as anyone who favored a more conciliatory solution, and calling for a push toward a socialist society. He also consistently urged an armed insurrection to overthrow the provisional government in the meetings of the Bolshevik Party.

In August of 1917, General Lavr Kornilov, Commander of the Russian army, joined with the Petrograd Soviet to undertake a military coup of the provisional government. The coup failed, but it did give the Bolsheviks the opportunity to push their socialist agenda back to the forefront. Their success was marked by the election of the Marxist Leon Trotsky to lead the Petrograd Soviets.

The success of the Bolshevik movement soon led to an armed expression of their revolutionary ideas. Lenin was instrumental in bringing about this next step. In October of 1917, militia loyal to the Bolsheviks took control of Petrograd's vital infrastructure, including transportation, communication, printing and utility assets in a bloodless coup. The Bolshevik party immediately declared the formation of a new government, with Lenin in the leading position of Chairman.

With his revolutionary goal achieved, Lenin led the new government, beginning by renaming the Bolshevik Russian Social Democratic Labor Party to the Russian Communist Party, thus emphasizing the goal of establishing a Communist society. He kept his campaign promise of peace by signing a diplomatic treaty with the Central Powers under harsh terms, and cancelling all of the commitments the Imperial government had made to its allies. This treaty worsened an already desperate situation in Russia, as the land lost to Germany was some of the most productive farmland in the famine gripped nation. In Lenin's mind, it was imperative that the new government move forward. With civil war between the

Bolshevik-led Red Army and the anti-Communist White Army growing, avoiding the continuation of a costly external war was worth almost any price.

With the new government installed and the threat of World War I addressed if not resolved, the pains inherent to shaping a new society continued. Peasant revolts in opposition to the Russian Communist Party's policies of war Communism were taking place all over Russia. At issue for the still-starving peasants was the forced requisition of their crops to feed the army and the people in the cities.

A revolt by the "Red Sailors" at the Kronstadt naval base added still more grievances. The sailors wanted free elections, freedom of speech, freedom of the press, freedom for peasants to manage their own lands, and the legalization of small businesses and industry. This naval uprising was put down with brutal efficiency by the Red Army under orders from Commissar Trotsky. The revolt was labelled a White Army plot by the Bolsheviks in power to avoid the compounding of outrage should the truth be made public. It was apparent that changes would need to be made.

Lenin implemented the New Economic Policy, or NEP, in March of 1921 in an effort to at once soothe the rebellious people and rebuild the Russian economy. The New Economic Policy was an interesting mix of socialism and capitalism. Many Bolshevik party members in government were against the policy and saw it as a betrayal of their communist goals. Lenin himself saw the policy as a temporary measure and called it the ante-chamber of socialism.

Under the New Economic Policy, the government maintained control of transportation, industry, and banking, but allowed private enterprise. People were able to build private businesses with their own restaurants, shops and industry. Peasants were allowed to work their own family farms. These measures allowed for the economy to begin its recovery quickly.

In other areas of society, measures were taken to improve life for all citizens in a controlled way. A literacy campaign was undertaken that provided instruction in traditional subjects as well as vocational training in an environment that promoted the government and communist ideas. Art and literature experienced a period of growth, even with the government censorship of all printed materials. Writers who strayed too far from approved Communist thought were at least rumored to disappear more often than reasonably expected.

Religion came under attack as counter to Communist ideas. Karl Marx had condemned religion in his writings as "the opiate of the people." On a more concrete level, the Russian Orthodox Church was closely associated with the czarist regime and had also been an ally of the anti-Communist White Army during the Russian Civil War. Nuns and priests were arrested and sent to labor camps while thousands of churches were destroyed. The Church that remained was under the control of the government, to the extent that some KGB officers even became priests as a means of infiltrating the religious culture.

Throughout all of this, the state-controlled media and printers created a kindly caretaker perception of Lenin. He was often referred to by the people as "Papa Lenin." Statues and busts of Lenin were erected in many Russian towns, and he would become a beloved leader in Russia to such an extent that, upon his death in January of 1924, his body was mummified to allow for public display in the Red Square mausoleum so that more mourners could view the body. The leader's body remains on display today in Moscow, where a group of scientists are assigned to maintain it in good condition.

# Trotsky

*"An army cannot be built without repression. The commander will always find it necessary to place the soldier between the possibility that death lies ahead and the certainty that it lies behind."*

—Leon Trotsky

Leon Trotsky, who would become head of the Petrograd Soviet and a leader in the Communist Party, started his career as a union organizer in Nikolayev. He would be in and out of prison and exiled repeatedly for his pro-Marxist activities until he finally became involved with the Bolshevik Party during the revolution. He became Lenin's second in command in the new government, one of seven men on the first Politburo. He was soon granted the title of Commissar for Foreign Affairs.

Oblivious to the upheaval in the Russian government, World War I continued to rage, with Russian forces faring poorly against their German foes. Trotsky reacted to the poor performance of the Russian military by determining it was impossible for their small, poorly trained and outfitted force to succeed against the German war machine. He advocated the creation of the Supreme Military Council to serve as an advisory body consisting of experienced Russian generals. This, in turn, led to the reorganizing and redirection of the Red Army under Trotsky as the new People's Commissar of Military and

Naval Affairs. He instituted policies of conscription, forced labor, and strict discipline. When peasants rose in opposition to the forced conscription into the Red Army, the common response from the conscription units was to force compliance. This was often done by taking family or friends as hostages and threatening to shoot them unless obeyed.

Trotsky would continue these policies and build upon them when he was appointed the People's Commissar of Army and Navy affairs. He spent the next several years transforming the disorganized and ineffective Red Army into a controlled and intimidating military force. One particular strategy had been particularly criticized: Trotsky utilized party-controlled blocking squads to manage inexperienced and conscripted troops in order to prevent them from fleeing battle or deserting.

Trotsky's leadership was essential to the revolutionary agenda. His tactics and organizational skills turned the Red Army into a fearsome military arm for the Communist Party. He believed in suppressing property owners and political opponents in order to promote socialistic government. Trotsky championed the use of concentration camps, labor camps, state control of trade unions, and summary executions. These practices would continue as state policy when Stalin took control of the government.

Trotsky's time as a political leader in Russia ended when he was pushed out by groups within the Communist Party who were critical of his techniques. Opponents cited his overreach in taking credit and failing to acknowledge the contributions others had made in the 1917 revolution. Having gone against directives from Lenin and Stalin, he was expelled from the Communist Party and deported from the Soviet Union.

Cut off from Russia, Trotsky endeavoured to support socialist movements in Mexico and the United States. He wrote several books during this time, giving his account of the events of the 1917 revolution and the development of Soviet Russia. He also tirelessly criticized the new leader of the Communist Party, Josef Stalin, and the totalitarian nature of his administration. His books were forbidden in Russia under Soviet regulations until 1987 and finally began to be published in his home country in 1989. He spent the last years of his life in exile and was finally murdered at his villa in Mexico by an agent employed by Stalin.

# October Revolution

*"It is true that liberty is precious- so precious that it must be rationed."*

—Lenin

The proletariat, as a social class, were described in Karl Marx and Friedrich Engel's Communist Manifesto as the industrial working class. The proletariat were seen as in direct opposition to the capitalist bourgeoisie, who were the traditional land and business owners. Marx believed that the overthrow of the bourgeoisie by the proletariat was fated; a natural evolution of society towards a classless society. With Bolshevik leaders who believed in the vision set forth in the Communist Manifesto, and the Russian working class growing more angry as their situation worsened, Marx's philosophy would soon be tested.

The Bolshevik party maneuvered and planned for the desired overthrow of first Imperial rule and then the provisional government at their headquarters in Petersburg and at the Smolny institute. They gained the support of the vast majority of the Russian army, and were making preparations in advance of the coming uprising, but the people were even more ready for revolution than anyone realized.

In March of 1917, the Russian workers of the proletariat took matters into their own hands. The scarcity of food had pushed them into desperate action.

Demonstrators took to the streets in Petrograd. Ninety thousand men and women joined in a general worker's strike, swelling the ranks of protestors to an overwhelming number. Police forces were unable to subdue the crowds, who took to rioting and destroying police stations throughout the city.

On March 11th, the troops stationed in Petrograd were ordered to take control of the uprising. Even though regiments of soldiers fired on groups of protestors, the people would not submit. When Czar Nicholas II responded by once again dissolving the elected legislative body, the Duma, the troops of the Petrograd garrison turned their support to the people.

With no support from the disbanded Duma, and no support from the Russian military, Czar Nicholas II found himself in an untenable situation. He officially abdicated the throne on behalf of himself and his young heir, Alexei. The people of Russia had forced an end to centuries of czarist rule without specific direction from the Bolshevik party and largely without bloodshed. The next target would be the provisional government.

# Execution

*"I pity the czar. I pity Russia. He is a poor and unhappy sovereign."*

—Sergei Witte, Russian Minister

After Czar Nicholas II abdicated the Russian throne in 1917, he and his family became little more than prisoners in the hands of first the Provisional Government under Alexander Kerensky and then the Bolshevik party and the Red Army. They were placed under house arrest, allegedly for their own protection, and frequently moved from house to house as the creation of a new government and the turmoil of civil war tore at Russia from the inside.

The family was treated increasingly poorly as time went on, and the lustre of Nicholas' previous position grew more tarnished in the eyes of revolutionary and war-weary men. The idea that he should be put on trial for crimes committed under his rule was a constant threat. The family was soon allowed fewer luxuries, servants and food, and were increasingly harassed by the soldiers assigned to guard their captivity. Bolshevik soldiers delighted in making lewd suggestions and drawing pictures on the fence to offend Nicholas' daughters.

The Bolsheviks had more to concern them than the imprisonment of one family. The White Army was opposed to the Red Army and the Bolshevik led Communist Party's control of the Russian government.

By July of 1918, White Army forces were getting uncomfortably close to Yekaterinburg, where the Romanov family was being held. The Bolsheviks knew they could not allow the family to fall into the hands of the White Army. Access to any one of the seven Romanov family members would legitimize the cause of the White Army in the eyes of many of the Russian people and, perhaps more importantly, other European governments, specifically the monarchies. The anti-Communist group would then be able to garner more powerful international support in their efforts to remove the Communist Party from power. This scenario had to be avoided at all costs.

Around midnight on July 17th, the Romanovs were informed by their guards that they were moving to a safer location. Relocation was a common occurrence throughout their captivity, so while the late night call to move was odd, it is likely the family was not unduly alarmed. They were told to wait in the small cellar of the house until their transport arrived.

After only a short wait in the dark room, they were surrounded by officers of the Secret Police. Yakov Yurovsky, the commandant charged with the family's care, read an official order aloud: "Nikolai Alexandrovich, in view of the fact that your relatives are continuing their attack on Soviet Russia, the Ural Executive Committee has decided to execute you." At this point, the small cellar became a chamber of death and terror as the execution squad opened fire. After the initial barrage, the doors were opened to allow the smoke to clear. Any of the Romanovs or their loyal staff members who were still alive were then bayoneted where they lay on the floor. It is believed this was the fate of the Romanov girls, Tatiana, Anastasia, and Maria. They appeared to have survived the shooting because the pounds of diamonds that had been secreted in their clothing gave them some protection from the bullets. The only Romanov son, fourteen-year-old Alexei, was shot twice in the back of his head.

The executioners hid the bodies, but because news of the royal family's deaths was advantageous to the Communist Party's cause, the actual deaths were not covered up. Treasonous correspondence between the Romanovs and imagined French allies was fabricated in order to justify the assassination.

Perhaps because of the mystery surrounding the location of the bodies of the executed royal family, a powerful legend arose. It was rumored, and perhaps hoped for among the Russian people, that Nicholas' daughter, Anastasia or his son Alexei had survived the massacre and gone into hiding. Several people stepped forward in the following years claiming to be one of those surviving children, some of them convincing enough to bolster the popular theory. This thin hope was renewed in 1991 when five bodies were exhumed from a pit covered with railroad ties along a lonely cart track north of Yekaterinburg. The bodies were identified using DNA comparisons as those of Czar Nicholas II, Czarina Alexandra, and three of the royal daughters. Two of the children were not found buried with the rest of the family, and it was eagerly viewed as evidence that both Alexei and Anastasia might have survived. Hope was shattered in

2007 when the bodies of Prince Alexei and his last sister were finally recovered and laid to rest with their family in the Saint Catherine Chapel in Saint Petersburg.

New information was released in 1993 with the report by one of the men responsible for maintaining the Romanovs' imprisonment, Commandant Yakov Yurovsky. The other men who took part in the execution were also identified as G.P. Nikulin, M.A. Medvedev, Peter Ermakov, S.P. Vaganov, A.G. Kabanov, P.S. Medvedev, V.N. Netrebin, and Y.M. Tselms. It is also noted that some of the guards refused to take part in the killing. Peter Voikov was the man charged with disposal of the bodies. He is recorded as having obtained one hundred and fifty gallons of gasoline and four hundred pounds of sulphuric acid from the Yekaterinburg pharmacy in the days surrounding the murders.

The date of the executions was documented as July 17th 1918. The curse Rasputin had placed on the family prior to his death in 1916 was finally chillingly proven to have been fulfilled. The family had indeed died just over the specified two years after Rasputin's own murder at the hands of Nicholas's relative. As to justice for the murdered family, the investigation into the deaths of Czar Nicholas II and his family was reopened in 2010 by a Moscow court as a case against the state, even though the men believed to be personally responsible had long since passed away.

# Stalin

*"I am especially distrustful of a Russian when he gets power into his hands. Not long ago a slave, he becomes the most unbridled despot as soon as he has the chance to become his neighbor's master."*

—Maxim Gorky

Josef Vissarionovich Djugashvili was a poor young man from Georgia. He suffered much from smallpox as a child, which left him with scars that would last his entire life. He managed to obtain a scholarship that allowed him to attend a seminary with the goal of becoming a priest in the Georgian Orthodox Church. While at school he began studying the works of the German philosopher Karl Marx and secretly supported the revolutionary movement to overthrow the Russian monarchy. He was actually expelled from the seminary for missing exams due to his work on Marxist propaganda.

With his education abruptly ended, Josef became a political agitator, and eventually joined the Bolshevik movement led by Vladimir Lenin. With his revolutionary activity including bank robberies, Josef was arrested and imprisoned multiple times between 1902 and 1913. When he was thirty years old, he changed his name to Joseph Stalin, from the Russian for "man of steel."

Stalin was a loyal member of the Bolshevik party. When Lenin was in exile in Switzerland in 1912, he appointed Stalin as the representative to the first Central Committee of the Bolshevik Party. When the Bolsheviks seized power in Russia from the provisional government set up after Nicholas II's abdication, Lenin was confirmed as the new leader. Stalin did well in the political environment thus created. He garnered more power in the party as the years went by, and in 1922 he became secretary-general of the Central Committee of the Communist Party. From this position, he maneuvered to raise his allies into positions of power as well. With this power base behind him, he was able to take control of the Communist Party after Lenin passed away in 1924. Within the decade, Josef Stalin would rule as dictator of the Soviet Union.

As one of his first acts as ruler, Stalin initiated a set of five-year plans meant to reshape the nation into a more profitable and manageable form. The government controlled the economy. The government collectivized and controlled the farms. The government controlled the media. The government controlled the police, and the government controlled the gulags, the forced labor camps. These policies did raise the agrarian Union of Soviet Socialist Republics into an industrial power, but the replacement of agricultural resources caused reduction in food supplies that contributed to the Soviet famine of 1932 and 1933.

When millions of farmers refused to turn over their farms and bow to government control, they were shot or exiled. The whole process of government takeover of the farms brought about a famine that spread throughout the Soviet Union. Millions of citizens died of starvation.

These actions were followed with the commencement of what is known as the "Great Purge." Between 1934 and 1939, members of the Communist Party, the military, and academic institutions who opposed or criticized Stalin and the Communist government were imprisoned, exiled or executed, often without a trial. Millions of people fell victim to this purge. Voices of dissent in Stalin's Soviet Union were silenced.

As a means of maintaining authority, Stalin increased the power of the state secret police and Soviet intelligence agencies in order to control the population. He also established a network of agents infiltrated in countries around the world, including Germany, Great Britain, Japan, France, and the United States.

In WWII, Stalin's government sided with the Allies against Nazi Germany and the Axis powers of Italy and Japan. The Soviet Union played a major role in the war with the Red Army defeating Nazi attempts at invasion and in the final capture of Berlin by Allied forces. With the loyalty established in the countries of the Eastern Bloc liberated by the Red army, the Soviet Union emerged from the war as a recognized world super power.

In post-war years, tension rose between the Soviet Union and Western nations, particularly the capitalist United States of America. This inflammatory relationship would be known as the Cold War, and worsened noticeably when the Soviet Union became the second nation in the world to develop nuclear weapons. Though the Cold War officially ended with the dissolution of the Soviet Union in 1991, relations between the nations of the former U.S.S.R. remain tenuous.

Stalin, the loyal Bolshevik who came to power in the aftermath of revolution, would rule Russia through the Second World War and the Korean War. He established a reign of terror that included executions, purges, labor camps and suppression. It is estimated he was responsible for the deaths of as many of twenty million people during his reign.

# Legacy

*"We Communists recognize only one sacred right – the right of the working man, his wife, and his child to live. We did not hesitate to wrest the land away from the landlords, to transfer the factories, mills, and railroads into the hands of the people..."*

—Leon Trotsky

The Russian Revolution of 1917 did not immediately lead to the global proletariat revolution that Bolshevik leaders expected and hoped for, but it did eventually change the world.

In 1944 during World War II, the lyrics of the Russian national anthem were changed to include a tribute to socialist leaders Lenin and Stalin. The new second verse reads: "Through tempests the sun of freedom shone to us, and the great Lenin illuminated our path. We were raised by Stalin to be true to the people. To labor and heroic deeds he inspired us!" After Stalin's death, these lyrics were no longer acceptable as a part of the national anthem. A new anthem was established in 2000, using the same music, but with no lyrics.

Numerous nations followed Russia in establishing Communist governments. Many of these nations made changes to their government, again following Russia's lead, after the Soviet Union was dissolved. Currently

China, Cuba, Laos, and Vietnam remain under communist regimes.

The ideas expressed by Karl Marx and Friedrich Engels in their Communist Manifesto have continued to be a force in socio-political thought throughout the years since its publication with Russian government. The Russian Revolution has been used as an example by both proponents and critics.

# Conclusion

*"If what you have done yesterday still looks big to you, you haven't done much today."*

—Mikhail Gorbachev

The Soviet Union dissolved in 1991, undone by a new popular revolution opposed to the government that had usurped the power of the Russian monarchy. The last leader of the Soviet Union, Mikhail Gorbachev, resigned and declared his office and title dissolved. All power in the government was turned over to Boris Yeltsin, the new Russian President. The fifteen Soviet Republics all seceded from the Soviet Union and became their own nations, struggling with instituting governmental structures of their own.

The statues of Lenin and Stalin that had stood for decades in town squares across the land were torn down one by one in a show of rebellion. The powerful cults of personality that had developed around these men in Soviet Russia lost some of their strength, but still maintain a hold on the hearts and minds of citizens of the dissolved nation. The heroes and sometimes villains of the revolution had themselves created a government as hated by the people as the monarchy had been in 1917, when Russia was remade by revolution.

54665598R00029

Made in the USA
San Bernardino, CA
22 October 2017